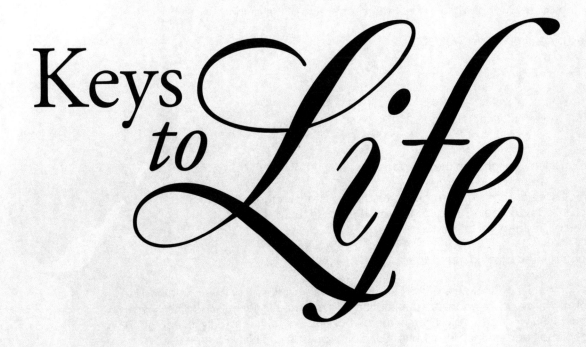

Keys to Life

AuthorHouse™
1663 Liberty Drive
Bloomington, IN 47403
www.authorhouse.com
Phone: 1 (800) 839-8640

Published by AuthorHouse 04/05/2018

ISBN: 978-1-5462-3575-0 (sc)
ISBN: 978-1-5462-3574-3 (e)

Library of Congress Control Number: 2018903996

Print information available on the last page.

This book is printed on acid-free paper.

authorHOUSE®

Keys to Life

*As Long as You're Open to Learn New Things,
the Teacher Will Always Appear*

Nathaniel Gawayne Sutton

In loving memory of my mother, Willie Mae Sutton, who always used to tell me, "With your mind, you can do anything."

In loving memory of my uncle Donald Hamilton Smith. He gave me the confidence to be me at all times.

To my loving wife, Savitri Sutton. Without her love and support, I could not dream as hard as I do.

Giving Thanks

Nathaniel Gawayne Sutton ©

My name is Nathaniel Gawayne Sutton; I was born in Newark, New Jersey, in 1961. My family moved to Plainfield, New Jersey, when I was about eight years old. I couldn't wait to get out of high school. It just wasn't a place I felt I could learn. I always felt as if what we were learning was all made-up and not important. History was just some man's story. I always new there had to be another way of learning.

But I always felt greatness, as if there was something inside me that I could not harness. When I would see people even when I was a young boy, I could sense people's inner emotions and sense if they were lying to me or telling me the truth.

I always felt that with my mind, I could change the way things would turn out. To me, thinking is not just a thing that rolls around in your head. Thinking is a power, a force of energy. The more you believe in something, the stronger it is. You have to understand that this world is more spiritual than physical. So we should trust our feelings more than our mind and what we see.

So I gave it a name; it's called having an inter-dimensional mind. To me, that means you have to believe that the universe we live in will teach us everything we need to know, as long as you keep a clean heart and mind. There are rules and laws in this place that we can't see. But the fact that the laws are there means life is more like playing chess than checkers.

I married the women of my dreams, Savitri. She's beautiful in every way. I own multiple real estate properties in New Jersey and New York. I'm an artist. I've won many art awards. I won the Award of Excellence from *Manhattan Arts International* magazine. I'm the author of the book *The Artist Known As Gawayne*. I'm an operating engineer for the state of New Jersey. I'm part owner, with Jill Lukasik, of a show German shepherd (Charles in Charge), who's won major dog shows. I'm a husband and father. My son, Wesley, is twenty-seven, with a great job and a great personality. He never asks for money, only advice. I'm a brother and an uncle. I feel I am living the dream. The only problem with the dream is that others can tell I can see something more than the average person sees. So my friends ask me questions about life. I don't mind. I'm thankful for the gift, so much so that I decided to write the most popular questions down and put them all in this book. And that's why I call it *Keys to Life*. I hope whoever reads it will not only get something out of it but will thoroughly enjoy it. Okay, enough small talk—let's get started.

I called the police

BE ME

. . . .

I had just lost my mother, the closes person to me. I was looking forward to a great job, the law and the academy. To almost everyone,it was the best I could ever be. But for me, it was not me, the law and the academy. So I prayed to God: should I be me or the law that I could no longer see? God said to me that what you want to be, anyone can be. So I said goodbye to the law and the academy. You see, I was born an artist, an artist is who I will always be, life after life … a gift from God to me!

By Gawayne 2003

Police officers, don't believe just because someone gives you a badge and gun, you have power over those who don't have them. Don't ever forget God's power and law. His law is the most powerful in the land (karma). It's alive everywhere. You can't run, and you can't hide behind a judge. If it doesn't get you in the beginning, it will always get you in the end. Respect and honor all lives.

If you go around hating the rich, that's one guarantee you will never become one of us!

Karma is real. You can't run from it, and you cant hide. It is always smart to do good things so that it can circulate back to you.

It's not how much money you make. Its how much _it_ costs you to make it!

When someone curses at you, try to focus on how they say it and not so much on what they say. If someone calls you the N word with a big smile on _their_ face and _their_ arms open to embrace you and they used it in a sentence, that's okay. But if they use the same word with a nasty look on their face as they turn away from you, it has a totally different meaning. It all depends on how people use their curse words!

You will never be able to control how much money you make, but you can always control how much you save.

If you never draw a line in the sand and say, "No more degrees and licensing in my life," and say, "It is what it is," you will never be happy.

There are only two kinds of children you will ever have. The first kind wants only their own. The second kind wants whatever you have. Once you realize you have the second kind of child, get them out of your pocket as fast as you can because when they grow up, you will see that one person cannot afford to take care of two adult people.

By the time your dreams catch up with your reality, you will already be in another dimension.

The only people who are truly free are the very, very rich. And the people who have absolutely nothing at all.

· ·

BEING A HUMAN BEING

A human being is one of the most uncertain things you can be. The only thing we are certain about is that we were born and we will one day die. We fall in love and sometimes cry. We never really know what we were put on earth for or what we were sent here to be. We are born and reborn again, a male or female, a human being. We are here to find the truth because only the truth can set us free, free from being a human being.

By Gawayne 2001

One Night

THREE LEVELS

....

I can look out over the land and see people with gifts coming from their hands. I can pick up a brush with little or no rush and make oil paint seem to blush. I now turn into the person God intended me to be—a great artist for all the world to see.

By Gawayne 2001

Every morning when we wake up, we should say to ourselves, "Today could be the best day of my life, or it could be the day I die!" Either way, you should thank the Creator for this amazing experience and such a wonderful journey.

There are so many rules and laws all around us that it takes years to learn them all. Some people learn a lot faster than others. That's why they excel much sooner than others. Or they just look much differently at what we call life.

My father looked at fatherhood a lot differently than most, or even all, fathers did. In his mind, as long as he gave you the tools to get what you wanted, he had done his job. Nothing wrong with that, but he had such a different approach.

My father never played catch with me in the yard or pushed me to play any sport. But when I turned seventeen, he took me to my uncle's bar, Ebony Manner, in Newark, New Jersey, and sat me at the bar, and told me to watch him very closely and listen to how he spoke and what he said. As he approached different women, he said, if you do just what I'm doing, you can have almost any woman you want. I liked the sound of that, so I paid close attention. And he was right; it works, and that is what I learned from it. You just have to let him or her know they are looking good without saying a word. Covered with smooth charm!

In my father's mind, most guys play catch in the yard to become good at sports so they can get on a team or possibly go to the pros so they can make a lot of money. Then, finally, they can get any woman they want!

Was my father wrong for not playing catch with me, or did he know and see a better, faster way of accomplishing the same goal?

Never judge your parents. It's not our job. Pay more attention to why they did what they did and less on what they actually did. And remember, they are children of God also, just a little older.

This society is set up for the rich to get richer and the poor to stay poor. Let me give you a few examples.

If you were to refinance your home to get a lower interest rate or go from a thirty-year mortgage to a fifteen-year mortgage, your mortgage company would have to call someone to appraise your home. Now, remember, you pay for the appraisal, but the bank contacts him and sends him to your house. Now, what your house is worth all depends on your appraiser's outcome. So, if the area you live in is middle class, it's so easy for the appraiser to say your property is not worth much more than you owe, regardless of your credit or income. Therefore, there is very limited growth you can gain out of this transaction, if any. But if you lived in Beverly Hills, the bank would trust you to pick the appraiser and give you fair market value for your property. Let me put it another way. If you lived in Beverly Hills or Las Vegas and you brought something you thought had a lot of value to a pawn shop, they would call in an expert to appraise your item. And if you wanted to sell it, that appraisal would be the determining factor in how much money you would make. Now, let's take that same item to Chicago or Detroit and walk into a pawn shop. There would be no expert coming, and no proper appraisal would take place. All they would say is if they like what you have and they want it, how much money do you need to help you out today? It's the same thing with a car. Mr. Middle Class tries to trade in his 2007 Chevy. Book value $10,000. They will only give you $7,000. Now you don't have as much as you thought you would have for your next vehicle. So that's three more thousand that are going to go on your next car. This is only one way Mr. Middle Class will end up paying more just to buy a new or newer used car. Mr. Beverley Hills buys a Porsche Cayenne. He drives it for a few years and goes to trade it in. For a new one! You best believe he will get book value for is a trade-in, mainly because he can go to any new Porsche dealer and get a fair deal, even by phone. It's all the same game. If a poor/working man owns it, it's not worth as much as you would like to think!

The only way I can see you getting around all three problems are as follows:

Bank refinance. Try to get their promise to you, in writing, before your property is appraised. Also, you should only have to pay for your appraisal at closing, not before. Always check agenthomevalues.com or Zillow first. Feel them out and wait until they honor their promise to you from the beginning. Make sure there's an appraisal corporation separate from the lender. That is your third party and your only protection from shady lenders.

Selling your items at pawn shops. If you see that the shop owner is not offering you a fair price for what you have, check eBay and see what your item *has* sold for, not what *it is* selling for. Do not hesitate; just leave go to another pawn shop. There are good, fair ones out there. Google one. You might have to travel to find one.

Car dealers. Always wait until the end of the month, when you know the dealer wants to sell as many cars as he can before the end of the month. Its always best if you can come with cash. Even a check from a bank or a credit union is much better than leaving the financing up to the dealer. Never negotiate by payment; that's an easy way for the dealer to overcharge you by stretching out your payments. Good luck.

Life on this planet is like going to Yale or Harvard because you come into this world without any memories of where you are from or who we are.

My father used to tell me everyone isn't paying with money, and my mother used to tell me other people are paying with sympathy and the rest are paying with kindness. You have to know the difference.

You haven't truly lived until you do something for someone so amazing that you make them cry. Drop down and thank God for your kindness.

Let's all be conscious of when we speak to our loved ones. We speak not with con and manipulation but with a clean and clear heart. Always put love first.

There is no such thing as your past; there is no such thing as your future. There is only the now. And you are, right now, that person you dream of becoming.

You are the only problem you will ever have. And you will always be your only solution to fix your problem.

Never be jealous of anyone. Because a man can be rich and miserable. And another man can be poor and happy.

If you mistreat a person who truly loves you, that's one guarantee the person you love will mistreat you.

Hard work can take you from A to B, but your imagination can take you everywhere.

Change in your life happens when the pain of staying the same becomes greater than the pain of making a change.

Most people's greatest fear is that they will fall. Your greatest fear should be that you will never know how it feels to fly.

The best thing we can do is look in the mirror! What holds us back is always looking out the window.

Its far more important for our children to have a high EQ than a high IQ. Unconditional love should always come first.

Whenever you're doing something new, make sure you're being pulled! Don't do it if you're feeling pushed!

You have to know you're special before others realize it.

Back in my day, when someone handed us garbage, we would put it in a green bag and throw it out back and put it in the trash. Today they would hand you the same garbage, put it on your dining room table, and tell you it's caviar!

When people are mean to you, you be kind to them. When they go low, you stay high! Keep your heart clean and ready for your next location!

The American eagle can live up to seventy years. But to reach this age, he must make a hard decision. In its fortieth year, its long claws can no longer grab his prey. His beak becomes bent. His feathers become old, thick, and heavy. He has two options, die or go through a painful process of change. He flies to the highest mountain. He then starts by knocking its beak against a rock until it's plucked out. Then he must pluck out his own claws, and then his old feathers. Afterward, everything grows back. He takes the greatest flight of his life, a rebirth, and he flies and lives for thirty more years. He had to change to survive and live!

I can remember a Father's Day. I had to be about sixteen or seventeen. I was sitting in a barber's chair, and the barber asked me what was I getting my fathers for Father's Day. I told him, "Nothing," even though I knew who my father was. He lived at home, with my family and me. He wasn't the kind of father I saw on television. Just then, two others kids said, "I don't know who my father is. I told my mother, 'When I grow up, I'm going to look for my father.'" His mother told him, "If you do, you may not like what you find." The other kid said, "I never saw a picture of a picture of my father." Just then, I felt thankful and appreciative of the father I do have. I got him a gift that year, and I never stopped. I think that we are too hard on our friends and family. We think they are supposed to be who we want them to be, while they can only be who they are!

When we are young, we see each other mostly at weddings. Now we only see each other only at funerals. It's the different stages of life, welcome it with open arms.

The greatest gift you can give yourself is to allow yourself to love and accept people just the way they are!

Just when you think you understand how things work, it's time to open your mind and accept that this may all be a lie!

I can remember telling my mother that the only fear I had was losing her. She told me it would be much better for me to lose her than it would be for her to lose me. That's the thinking of a real mother. What a lady. What a woman.

If you feel you don't have the money you should have, save up and take a rich person out to dinner, just to hear what he or she talks about.

You are never completely apart of someone else until you help them make their dreams come true!

To complete your life's journey, you must focus on your deeds. The most important deeds are at the time you do the deed. You must know that if you guys could change places, they would not do the same for you.

Life is all about what we have that's priceless and we give it away, not what we receive that's priceless and we keep!

What do you call a man who creates his own symbol? I would die for you. Half-black and half-male. You got the look. Concerned with chem trails. "Purple Rain." He filtered his water to stay alert so the thieves in the temple wouldn't steal his masters. What do you call a man who makes you aware of the signs of the times? Tells you that you are as precious as diamonds and pearls. If you drive a red Corvette, you need to slow down. He reminds us that we all are running out of time. 1999. A singer, multi-instrumentalist, producer-actor, and renowned innovator. I call him what he is, the son of the king. His Royal Highness, Prince. R.I.P.

We look up to say hello. We set down to learn. We stand up to play the game. We move to dance. We lean backward to laugh. We kneel down to pray. We lie down to say goodbye.

Whenever you see beauty, compliment beauty. Whenever you see kindness, return kindness. Whenever you see love, give love in return. This is God expressing himself through you and as you.

There are five things we can do to give our lives longevity.

1. Keep a quiet, clean heart.
2. Always sit like a tortoise.
3. Walk proud like a pigeon.
4. Work like a horse.
5. The most important: learn to sleep like a dog.

Gentleman, it's much easier to become a big fish if you first catch a big fish.

Did you know you could live life and never get old, never be hungry, never feel poor, and have the ability to solve all problems? All you have to do is just love someone unconditionally and be loved unconditionally in return, and the world is yours!

When God gives us the gift of being beautiful, it has nothing to do with our appearance. It has to do with how others view us when we interact with others. Remember, the greatest thing you can do on this earth is to make someone smile.

We come into this world, and by the time we realize who we are and who truly loves us, one by one, they slowly leave us here alone. We struggle to live on as if everything is okay, waiting for our day to reunite at the next location!

A real friend always brings up your strengths, constantly shows you different ways you can use them, and always reminds you not to waste them. Friends like that are a gift from God!

The best kind of people are the ones who come into your life who believe in you so much that you start believing in yourself!

Did you know, the lower your IQ, the more you need a lot of people to have a good time? So the next time it's a Friday or Saturday night, and everything you love is right in front of you but you still feel the need to find a party, it's time to grow up. There's nothing wrong with being alone. It does not mean you're lonely.

It's so easy to feel invincible when everything is going your way. In life, it is a true challenge is to feel invincible when the world around you is falling apart.

The only thing we have complete control over in life is our attitude. If we don't learn to control it, it will control our quality of life.

Sometimes when we say nothing, we can be heard loud and clear. No one can make us feel as good as a kind word from someone who has hurt us in the past. This is just a small trip in a lifetime journey!

It's a normal thing to make new friends and lose the old one. The more you grow, the more old friends will say you have changed. The only problem is old friends who are not willing to grow.

In life, the only two people you will never forget. Will be your first love and your last. Usually, its because they were truly in love with you.

You know you're rich! Not when you have millions of dollars, not when you can buy a new car. You know you're rich not when you make six figures, not when you live in a big house. Always remember this. You know you're rich whenever you can keep your refrigerator full!

You can never get as angry as someone you made angry, especially if they didn't want to get angry! Only treat people the way you want to be treated.

If you thought education was expensive, wait until you see what ignorance will cost you.

The next time you see one of your loved ones, really see them. Look them all over, up and down. Talk to them looking directly in their eyes. Remember, you can see them far better then they can ever see themselves. Once they're gone from this planet, you can never see them in person again.

Small-minded people are so predictable. If you text them for help and they don't respond, just text them back and tell them you have something they want and see how fast they text or call you back.

There are three levels of spiritual development. At the first level, you can see a miracle. At the second level, you can create a miracle. At the third and final level, you become a miracle.

I believe there are about twenty-six different versions of the bible. Countless churches and so many different beliefs. If, for some reason, you don't believe that the choices we make, how we treat one another, even how giving we are, determines where we go after we die, you're only kidding yourself. Stop following the reality shows and start following your inner voice!

Most people think gold is the most precious substance on earth. But the truth is that love is. I know you cant see it or touch it. Just because you cant see something, that doesn't mean it's not real. I can prove it. It's the only thing you can take with you after you pass on. Don't ever take love for granted, because it's almost impossible to jump start after it's gone!

Let's get back to doing what our parents did and we did when we were young. Find some music and go dancing. Dancing relieves stress, improves memory, and improves flexibility. One more thing. When you dance with someone special, you will never forget that night.

People can't read your mind, but they can feel what you are thinking. The next time you have to speak to someone you don't care for, try to remember they are only human and are probably doing the best they can. So just smile because it's hard to smile and think nasty at the same time.

Do you know someone, a friend or maybe a family member, who has been kind to you in the past? Do you want to do something special for them? Mail them a gift or even money. But don't let them know you sent it. Never tell them. Now that's sowing a seed.

Some people don't believe that the earth and nature is alive. Really alive. The next time someone does something wrong to you or says something inappropriate, don't do or say anything. Let the universe deal with them. It's called fighting without fighting. Try it. Just give it time!

To all the single ladies that want to get married, once you pick out the guy, you would like to married.

Whatever you do with him, don't have sex with him until he tells you he loves you and he wants to spend the rest of his life with you. He's all yours after that. Good luck!

Have you ever wanted to motivate someone, inspire them to mutate into a better person, force them to transform into whatever they may dream of? All you have to do is laugh in their face and tell them there's no way they can change!

Have you ever had a long-time friend who's always telling people you're their good friend but every time you look around, they're always doing something weird or creepy behind your back. I say get rid of them and make room for other decent people who want to be in your life. Just because you guys have been friends for years, that does not mean they're your friend, especially if you don't feel it.

Poor people will always judge you by how much money you make. Rich people will always judge you by how much money you have. But God and his angels will only judge you by how much money you gave away!

To educate a five-year-old child, all you have to do is teach them how to think. It should take about twenty-four hours. But to completely program them, it will take about twelve years or more!

There's a big differences between being smart and thinking you're smart. If you ever have to decide between being kind or being right, always choose to be kind, and I guarantee you that you will be right every single time!

Have you ever walked by one of your loved ones, your wife or husband or maybe one of your children, and felt like giving them a big kiss or hug, but you didn't, because it wasn't the normal time you show affection? The next time you feel it, go for it. You will be giving them something they will never forget!

In the game we call life, do not waste your life waiting until you die to realize it was all a game. No matter where you are, you are always on stage, and you will always have an audience. And it's completely up to you what role you play. That's why it's called the game of life!

The most important two words in anyone's vocabulary should be "thank you." By not saying these two words, two things are guaranteed to happen. One, you will hurt the feelings of the first party. Two, the first party will never be so kind to you again!

If you know you're smarter than someone, you should be smart enough never to let them know.

You may think it's very difficult to find out if the person you're with is really the right one for you. But it's really very easy to find out. If you start to lose things you always had, you're with the wrong person. But if you start getting things you never had, you're with the right person. It's really that easy.

Soul mates are real. The eyes are the windows to the soul, maybe from another time, world, or space. You guys spent a lot of time together. From the first time your eyes meet, you will never forget the location, the words that were said, and most of all, the feelings you both felt. Strangely, for the rest of your life, here on earth, every time you think of each other, you will never be able to turn that feeling off.

Having a job is a good thing. The definition of job is "just over broke." The only way you can get ahead of having a job is to get paid with gold, silver, or diamonds.

It's much better to overpay for the right thing than it is to get the wrong thing for half price.

If we are truly friends, we should feel free to voice our opinion (argue) and not feel any fear of any of it leaking through into our tomorrow's experience.

You can teach a person to sing, and you can teach a person to dance, but to teach a person to think is the greatest gift in the land!

We are programed to see death when we look at a dead body. What we should see is life, like a caterpillar turning into a butterfly. No sadness. It's a celebration! (Row, row, row your boat gently down the stream, merrily, merrily, merrily, merrily, life is but a dream)!

Things that were downloaded into me during my time here on earth:

There is no such thing as Santa Claus. Einstein was not a genius. African Americans are not from Africa. The earth is not round. We don't vote presidents into office. The government controls the weather. Racism is taught. There is nothing free. Aliens are real. We are all aliens; we come from different planets. Our bodies we walk around with are our space suits. Your name is a small time capsule in the lifespan of your journey. Everyone's heaven is on a different planet. Life on earth is school. The matrix is real. Avatar is real. Dinosaurs are still alive. The newscasters are paid by the rich to tell the middle class to blame all their problems on the poor. The worst thing you can do to your body is take medicine. The female is the head of every household. We are already microchipped (iPhones). People who you think have money don't! The people who you don't think have money do!

The majority of middle-class people are paying into their unions to protect their employers from them. A large percentage of inmates in prison today were gated to their cells from birth, by pouring drugs intentionally into poor neighborhoods and also by their lack of education due to underpaid teachers and crowded classrooms in their communities. We must show more mercy toward our fellow humans entering into this world. The reason for life itself is for all people to find God and to create an establish a loving relationship with him directly. It's called finding the truth because only the truth can set you free, free from what you may ask, free of being born and reborn again. Only the truth can set you free!

What you don't learn in this life: You will return to learn it and get it right. This is school; your real world awaits you. Enjoy every minute of your journey!

Amen and God bless you always

Hour Glass

Traveling through the sands of time.Sand down the hour glass.The egyptian pharaoh's knew from the very beginning the after life holds the crown.Sand down the hour glass, your name a mere time capsule through space and time.Live rich than poor.Male than female ,hot than cold never to really know what we were born for.To give from your heart not your mind ,sand down the hour glass. To love and to be loved.Crawl walk sit in a chair than a wheel chair .Born and reborn again sand down the hour glass, to be dark than light all seven cards dealt in delight different suits to be played.A test or practice for a world our eyes and minds not yet prepared for.Judged on attitude towards all problems and events may you neal down before the Source and allow the crown to find its place before all the sands run down the hour glass...!

by nathaniel Gawayne Sutton
2015

17

Father Time

Nanny

You and I

Love Me

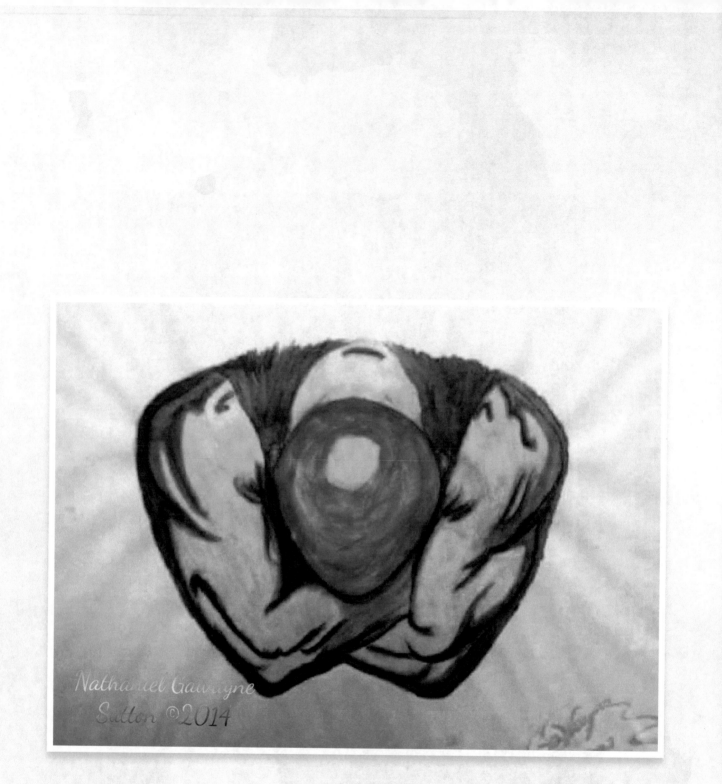

Deep Thought

Nathaniel Gawayne
Sutton ©

Back together again

Paradise

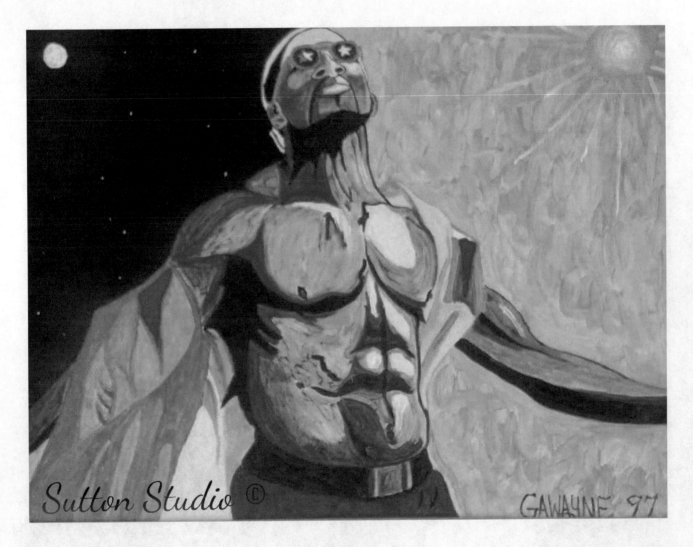

Reborn

A Time to Pray

Dancing in the dimensions

Last Letter

Letting Go

Muhammad Ali and Myself

My Dog Charles in charge as a puppy

My History

My One and Only Son

Gawayne

My Charlie

My Son, Wife and myself

My Son

My wife and I

Gawayne

Mother of justice

My wife and I

My wife and I

Printed in the United States
By Bookmasters